LADY DEALER

By Martha Watson Allpress

Lady Dealer premiered at the Edinburgh Festival Fringe in August 2023 at Paines Plough's Roundabout at Summerhall, produced by Grace Dickson Productions and directed by Emily Aboud.

LADY DEALER

By Martha Watson Allpress

The team for the Edinburgh Fringe 2023 production of *Lady Dealer* were:

Charly   Alexa Davies

Writer   Martha Watson Allpress
Director   Emily Aboud
Sound Designer   Anna Short
Lighting Designer   Jonathan Chan
Set & Costume Designer   Blythe Brett
Dramaturg   Lizzie Manwaring
Stage Manager   Nikita Bala
Production Manager   Ethan Hudson
                                for Frontseat Media

Producer   Grace Dickson
Assistant Producer   Rory Thomas-Howes

Martha Watson Allpress

Martha Watson Allpress is a writer and actor from Lincolnshire in the East Midlands. Her debut play, *Patricia Gets Ready (for a date with the man that used to hit her)*, sold out its 2021 run at the Edinburgh Fringe and received 5-star reviews from the *Guardian*, The Stage, Broadway World and others. Her second play, *Kick*, won the Bill Cashmore Award and had a limited run at the Lyric Hammersmith. At the end of 2022 she worked with Kestrel Theatre Company to write a Christmas show, *The Christmas What Got Forgot*, with and for the residents of HMP Springhill, which they then performed for friends and family. As a screenwriter Martha is developing original ideas with Various Artists Ltd and Red Planet Pictures.

Emily Aboud

Emily Aboud is a Trinidadian theatre director. She was shortlisted for the JMK Award in 2022 and 2021. She is a recipient of the Evening Standard Future Theatre Award. Recent credits include *Splintered*, which she also wrote(Soho Theatre Main House), *Close Quarters* (LAMDA); *Salt Slow* (RCSSD); *Bogeyman* (Edinburgh Fringe 2022, also writer); *Pink Lemonade* (Bush Theatre); *Dolly* (Park Theatre) and *Chatham House Rules* (Pleasance Theatre). As a Caribbean theatremaker, her work draws inspiration from the political community theatre she grew up making in Trinidad – a combination of music, movement, direct audience address and theatricality.

Anna Short

Anna trained at LAMDA. Theatre credits as Sound Designer include *Spy for Spy* (Riverside Studios); *Primary Shakespeare: As You Like It*, *Seven Celebrations* (Orange Tree Theatre); *Crackers* (Polka Theatre); *Ravenscourt* (Hampstead Theatre); *Press/4* (Park Theatre); *Don't*

Smoke in Bed (VAULT); *Nothing on Earth* (UK Tour); *In This Smoking Chaos* (Queen's Theatre Hornchurch); *Camp Albion* (Watermill Theatre/UK Tour); *I Know I Know I Know* (Southwark Playhouse); *The Straw Chair* (Finborough Theatre).

As Co-Sound Designer: *Get Happy* (Pleasance Theatre).

As Associate Sound Designer: *My Son's a Queer (But What Can You Do?)* (Turbine Theatre); *Folk* (Hampstead Theatre); *Lesbian Space Crime* (Soho Theatre); *Two Billion Beats* (Orange Tree Theatre).

Jonathan Chan

Jonathan trained at the Guildhall School of Music and Drama. His credits include: *Grindr: The Opera* (Union), *Snowflakes* (Park & Old Red Lion); *All Roads* (London Tour); *Get Happy* (Pleasance); *Emmeline* (UK Tour); *In the Net* (Jermyn Street); *Grandad Me and Teddy Too* (Polka); *The Solid Life of Sugar Water* (Orange Tree); *Heroin to Hero* (Edinburgh Fringe); *Move Fast and Break Things* (Camden People's Theatre and Edinburgh Fringe); *Pussycat in Memory of Darkness, The Straw Chair* (Finborough); *Maybe Probably, Belvedere* (Old Red Lion); *Different Owners at Sunrise* (The Roundhouse); *Barstools to Broadway, Amphibian* (King's Head); *Sticks & Stones, Time, Random* (Tristan Bates Theatre); *Urinetown: the Musical, Opera Makers* (Guildhall School); *Fidelio* (Glyndebourne – Assistant Lighting Designer) and *The Passenger* R&D (Guildhall – Associate Lighting Designer).

Blythe Brett

Blythe is a performance designer and theatre collaborator. She trained at the Royal Welsh College of Music and Drama, graduating in 2020. Recent designs include *Project Dictator* (New Diorama Theatre); *Who Killed My Father* (Tron Theatre); *Three Sisters* (LAMDA); *Get Happy*

(Pleasance London) and *Ariadne* (English Touring Opera). Blythe is a recipient of the Linbury Prize for Stage Design 2021 and Lord Williams Memorial Prize for Design 2020.

Lizzie Manwaring

Directing credits include: *Lord Of The Flies* (LIPA), *Bible John* (Edinburgh Fringe 2019 and VAULT Festival 2020 – Pleasance Charlie Hartill Recipient); *The Woman Who Gave Birth To A Goat* (Camden People's Theatre); *WAGGO* (Edinburgh Fringe 2017) and *And Then...* (Latitude Festival).

Associate Directing credits include: *RuneSical* (Edinburgh Fringe 2022).

Assistant Directing credits include: *Vardy v Rooney: The Wagatha Christie Trial* (West End – Ambassador's Theatre and Wyndhams); *Maria Stuart* (Schauspiel Stuttgart); *The Two-Character Play*, *The Dumb Waiter* (Hampstead Theatre); *The Tyler Sisters*, *Unknown Rivers* (Hampstead Downstairs); *Too Clever By Half* (Rose Bruford) and *A New And Better You* (Yard Theatre).

Dramaturgy credits include: *The Glass Ceiling Beneath The Stars* (Edinburgh Fringe 2023)

Alexa Davies

Alexa's breakthrough role was in the 2012 British comedy film *Vinyl*, written and directed by Sara Sugarman. Alexa went on to play Aretha in two series of Channel 4's *Raised by Wolves* and joined the cast of the BAFTA-winning comedy *The Detectorists*, written, directed by and starring Mackenzie Crook. She could also be seen as Betsey Fletcher in Hulu's *Harlots* and in *Mamma Mia! Here We Go Again* as Young Rosie. Alexa has played a leading role in two series of *Dead Pixels* for E4 and also starred in *Misbehaviour*, a British comedy-drama film directed by

Philippa Lowthorpe. She could be seen in *White House Farm* for ITV and *Honour* for Vera Pictures. She appeared as series regular Marj in the comedy drama *Funny Woman* based on the novel *Funny Girl* by Nick Hornby, as well as the third series of *Cobra,* both for SKY.

Grace Dickson Productions is a bold new production company, developing and producing formally innovative and bitingly relevant new writing that champions marginalised voices. GDP works collaboratively with artists on professional development as well as producing work that isn't afraid to make a noise and ruffle some feathers. GDP produces theatre that represents the world we live in and the worlds beyond it; work that is imaginative, playful and boundary-breaking. Previous collaborations include Rhum + Clay, The REcreate Agency, Park Theatre, Bric A Brac, Freight Theatre, Ransack Theatre & Silent Faces, at venues such as Park Theatre, New Diorama, Soho Theatre, Southwark Playhouse, Roundhouse and on tour.

GDP encompasses the work of Grace Dickson, a Newcastle-born producer with a keen eye for powerful, socially relevant new writing. Grace works across the industry in roles including Associate Producer at Francesca Moody Productions (*An Oak Tree, Kathy and Stella Solve A Murder, Feeling Afraid As If Something Terrible Is Going To Happen*), Company Producer for Lagahoo Productions and These Girls, Accounts Assistant/Bookkeeper at Runaway Entertainment and co-founder of HD General Management with Ameena Hamid. Her recent work is supported by the Stage One Bursary for New Producers.

Credits include *Lady Dealer* (Roundabout, Edinburgh Fringe), *Glass Ceiling Beneath The Stars* (Pleasance,

Edinburgh Fringe) with Bric a Brac Theatre, *Summer Camp for Broken People* (Summerhall, Edinburgh Fringe) with The REcreate Agency, *SPLINTERED* (Soho Theatre), *Project Dictator* (New Diorama), *Move Fast and Break Things* (Summerhall, Edinburgh Fringe), *BOGEYMAN* (Pleasance Edinburgh Fringe), *Flushed* (Park Theatre) and *Belly Up* (Turbine Theatre).

www.gracedicksonproductions.co.uk
@gdicksonprods

With phenomenal thanks to:

Grace Dickson, Emily Aboud, Lizzie Manwaring, Alexa Davies, Anna Short, Jonathan Chan, Blythe Brett, Nikita Bala, Ethan Hudson and Rory Thomas-Howes.

Mark Cartwright, Tristan Baker, Francesca Moody, Eleanor Lloyd, Kater Gordon, Louise Goodman, Ros Brooke-Taylor, Fraser Dickson, Alison Wardropper, Ameena Hamid, and the whole team at Paines Plough.

LAMDA, Lyric Hammersmith, Open Door and Hackney Showroom.

Amy Sparks, Alessandra Davison and Freya Bateson.

Adam Isla O'Brien, Ernest Kingsley Jnr, Tom Claxton, Simon Tait and Zachary Willis.

Dexter Flanders, Jessica Norman, Magda Bird, Mary Clapp, Nancy Netherwood, Nic McQuillan, Nicola Taylor, Patrick Swain, Phoebe Frances Brown, Sarah Power and Sid Sagar.

M.W.A.

LADY DEALER

Martha Watson Allpress

Character

CHARLY, *late twenties. Gobby. Probably would've lazily been called a 'tomboy' at school. Well read. Smart. Has absolutely no interest in you and your life. Knowingly moves big and speaks big, so you don't see the littleness inside her.*

Notes

The script can be minimally altered to account for the accent/home of the actor playing Charly. Preferably Charly is from South London/Essex. Charly must not have an RP accent.

Charly cannot stop, else she feels it all.

Whilst the 'I am fine's do not need to be exact in number, they do need to go on meaningfully longer than expected. Push past the instinct to stop. Say it, keep saying it, want to stop, and keep going. And keep going. And keep going. And keep going. And keep going. And keep going. And keep going.

Underlined text indicates it is not Charly speaking, however, it is at the director's discretion how this is conveyed.

This text went to press before the end of rehearsals and so may differ slightly from the play as performed.

There is the intro to 'Sabotage' by Beastie Boys. Always heading up and up, crescendoing constantly to a climax it never reaches. There is only the intro. There is only noise.

There is also a hum of weed.

There is also a baby crying. There is also the bitter taste of bile. There is also the stench of decade-old-vomit. There is also the cackle of teenage laughter. There are also friends that aren't friendly. There is also the abyss of a lover. There is also the phrase 'class-traitor'. There is also a father who doesn't exist. There is also a mother who exists a bit too much. There is also a country that genuinely sucks balls. There is also the sound of cash rubbing against cash. There are also unsayable words. There is also the NHS. There is also climate change, income inequality and the fact that that singer cheated on that actor. There is also Ezra Collective. There is also an argument five doors down. There is also the noise of a fast-food chain that only exists in that fast-food chain. There are also too many people. There is also China's solution to that. There is also your phone. There is also the news. There is also fast fashion. There is also your bank.

There is also more.

There is also more. There is also more.

CHARLY *wakes up.*

CHARLY *steadies her breath.*

She is fine. She is fine. She is fine.

It takes as long as it takes.

She dry-retches. She swallows it.

Then she entirely changes who she is.

CHARLY.

I wake up.

I wake up wondering if today is going to be the same.

And it will.

But it's nice to play that game. Gonna grow up eventually but not today because today will be the same.

Sure, I could aim higher than the high guy but why would I do that when today feels like yesterday and yesterday was what it was what it was what it was. Coz. My days have structure. I'm not trying to piss on my days, like, they're not bad. But basically, being me involves a lot of the same. Surely you can relate. The mundanity of a day keeps us all safe. Sudden digressions of the norm reform reshape the butterfly effect. I've seen that film; I'm not trying to die. Or lose an arm. I am happy to make out with Amy Smart, but that's not the point.

The point is, I am fine, and today is going to be the same.

Sure, if I did things different it would be different. But I don't and I won't coz I can't so it's not. Are you following? I'm swallowing my pride here, guys. I'm trying to explain, that today is going to be the same and that's okay. That's good. So it should. Sorted. So. I should continue.

Right?

Dare ya.

I wake up.

PS – if the rhyming thing gets boring, like if I begin to hear hints of snoring, then I'll cut it out. That's not what this is about, it's just… you'll get it. It dies.

Dramatic.

Okay. So.

I wake up. Cripplingly aware I've said that three times, but for clarification it has only happened once. Today. Obviously happened more than once in my lifetime. God. Right. Okay.

I wake up – four – that's how it starts. That's how it always starts.

It last ended when I suspended my awake-ness. I fell asleep when the sun came up, so now I'm starting late. Which I do every day. Last out the gate. Got to get up early once in my life to see the sunrise kiss the sky, but that's usually when I'm winding down. Don't appreciate the hazy orange pink big blue when you're carrying twenty-four hours of weight with you. But I'm up now and it's chill. You need to chill. Everyone needs to chill.

She allows a breath.

Chalk it up to nerves.

My foggy eyes take in my bedroom. Latching onto different inanimate objects that tell me I'm alive. Ticking them off in my misty mind; bookcase, dildo, poster, window...

I had a break-up not too long ago, so some signs of the hoe live on. The fairy lights hung at the foot of my bed. That's her. That's her all over. By the way, hoe ain't derogatory – yeah, I say words like derogatory – but hoe ain't derogatory, especially if I'm saying it. It's affectionate. I'm probably still the inspiration for her metaphorical morning glory. Glorious. And she's my inspiration for the gory dreams I wake up from sweating. Blood blowing out all of her orifices. Prick.

I'm not bitter.

At all.

It was amicable.

We amicably agreed that she was allowed to devastate me.

Amicably, I spent a week dining exclusively on cold baked beans and very aggressive porn.

Things that break: storms, hearts, condoms. Smart to know that going in. Pun intended. But I am mended. I'm not bitter.

I'm fine. I'm over her. Amicably over and over and over and –

She coughs and splutters.

My respiratory system takes a minute to stabilise. Same for my eyes, I'm still taking in my bedroom. Guys, it's nothing… special? I mean it's mine. I like it coz it's mine. And shit I haven't kept the fairy lights as a weird little shrine. Like me and Clo – the hoe – she and I will always be entwined, but she's the kind that takes to the Alpines, living off Daddy's goldmine. I was her rebellion. Or at least I would've been if she'd ever have let me meet her family. Instead, I'm an anecdote now. Embellished no doubt. They'll laugh about me over dinner parties in years to come. They'll have dinner parties. I mean that's a trip, to be a blip on someone's record. To exist purely as an anomaly. I'm over her. I don't mind. But my room is mine.

Fuck refined.

My room is ratchet. Like me. Raggedy and likeable? I think. It has the look of 'freshly departed from parents', but it's been mine for a while now. Just mine. Silly cow mother implemented a no-laundry policy aged eighteen. Depressingly long ago, no matter how much I will it nearer. Do I? Maybe not. And thus, the tower. The tower in the tower block feels like it's honouring something. Honestly though it's just an architectural structure of laziness. A tower of fast fashion I slowly gave up on. A Jenga of T-shirts and joggers crusty with sweat and exhaustion and maybe some other unmentionable stuff.

Somewhere within that, there is a pastel-yellow jumper. Not mine.

It will topple eventually.

Over and over and over and –

Not content with building the Barbican, I made the Twin Towers, and next to my laundry pile is another column: books. All read. All dusty. All unloved and adored. The dried-up pages spooning each other recalling the last time they were caressed by skin. Me and them have that in common. Curious my reluctance to chuck them away when they're done with… but… they're mine. Top of the pile, and most recently satisfied; you're welcome, lads; is *Widow Basquiat* by Jennifer Clement. Bit indulgent but who the fuck wouldn't. I should donate them somewhere. Where? What'd be the point? What's the point?

I'm up. Five. Nearly.

With great UGH I throw my legs out of my bed. I can't lie my head hurts horribly, hopefully momentary.

She waits.

Yup.

I'm fine.

If we follow the nursery rhyme down – head, hurts, shoulders, tense, knees, bent and toes now planted in a day-old pizza box. BBQ Texas. Don't judge me. This moment will not shame me. I mean it didn't yesterday. And today will be the same. At least there's no fucking pineapple in sight. Some social lines cannot be crossed, and I understand that. It will not shame me. You cannot shame me.

I should name me.

I'm Charly.

Good morning.

Today is going to be the same.

My marinara-coated extremities flex to support all my weight. And the rest.

Put simply, for the simple among us, I stand up. I meander out of the boudoir. That's right, boudoir. I'm fancy. French. Fucking stoned still. Okay. Into the kitchen for a good dose of coffee.

Put it in my veins. And then? Then we'll begin the day that is going to be the same.

The kettle boils over and over and over and –

Something in the aggression of the boiling kettle matches the rhythm inside me. I choose not to dwell on it. Don't dwell, Charly. You're not you without a coffee.

Who the fuck are you without your coffee?

Me, well, I'm less ladylike. Less lovely, let's be literal, I'm less fucking human. Humdinger to admit the necessity of caffeine to function but there are worse things to be addicted to. Oooh. Bad rabbit hole. Let's not. Nobody needs that. Nope. Nah. I'm an instant lass. I know folks get gassed about buying beans, burning them on a stovetop heirloom. Not me. Two teaspoons of instant and instantly –

She sips her coffee in the quiet.

The quiet changes the world.

It's lonelier.

Alright well that's enough of that. You get the idea.

You're searching for a rhyme, it's not coming. I'm letting you down. I thought I should just do that early on, get it out the way, so you don't harbour unreal expectations about me. Yeah?

I'm a person.

Oh well.

Sip. More quiet. Back to...

What?

Sip. More quiet. Back to...

What?

Sip. More quiet. Back to...

WHAT?!

Sip. More quiet. Back to…

Ah you know what, yeah, fuck this.

Exasperated and angered she turns on some music.

'Sabotage' – Beastie Boys.

She plays it far too loud and shouts over it.

THIS IS HOW WE BEGIN THE DAY THE SAME.

I WENT TO A PARTY ONCE, A POSH UNIVERSTIY
ONE. THEY PLAYED LOADS OF BEASTIE BOYS.
BLESS THEM I GUESS THAT WAS REALLY THEM
TRYING TO GET IT. UNDERSTAND SOMETHING
OTHER THAN THEMSELVES, BUT YA KNOW. IT'S
THREE POSH BOYS FIGHTING FOR A RIGHT THEY
ALREADY HAD. I'M NOT – I LIKE IT – I HADN'T
REALLY HEARD ANY OF THEIR STUFF BEFORE
AT ALL SO IT WAS A BIT LIKE BIT OF A FUCKING
HEADFUCK. IT WAS JUST IN THE BACKGROUND
BUT I'M NOT GOOD AT CONVERSATIONS AT PARTIES
SO I TUNED INTO IT. I LIKED IT. THEY WERE
PLAYING *PAUL'S BOUTIQUE* BUT I WENT HOME AND
I LISTENED TO *LICENSE TO ILL…* BECAUSE WHEN
YOU GOOGLE THEM, THAT'S WHAT COMES UP
INNIT. THAT'S THE EASY STUFF. SO THAT'S WHAT I
LISTENED TO. ADAM YAUCH WOULD'VE TOTALLY
GOTTEN IT. AND LIKE YEAH THEY'RE NOT PERFECT
AND NOT FOR EVERYONE BUT IT'S LIKE –

The music abruptly cuts out.

CHARLY *walks over to, hits and fiddles with the PA system.*

The music doesn't return.

Whatever.

Coffee's kicked in. I don't need them anyways. Don't need
anyone. Which is fortunate. Because – um –

She necks the remainder of her coffee.

LET'S GO MOTHERFUCKERS.

So, one thing to explain. One piece of vital information. Yeah? I am a trailblazer. I am an icon. I am… a female drug dealer.

Look I know it's not exactly what you want to encourage your little babies to be doing, but fact of the matter is it's good money, and someone does have to do it, you know. Now, why the only options for that someone is Top Boy or Tory Private Doctor… never made no sense to me. You just need a gravitas and a positive attitude. And no, maybe I'll never make Forbes 30 Under 30, and, alas, no unions, but I run a good, ethical – ish – business. Proper homegrown, mate, authentic, Whole Foods-type drugs.

I'm fucking with ya, I get them from my lad in Eltham but not had any deaths or complaints so – can't complain if you're dead suppose – it started in uni. I went to a good one – the best one… yeah… that one. Smart hoe, you know. But I sound like I do, so at every party – which weren't parties PS, they were literally dull as hell, they were closer to political parties than a fucking rave – but at these parties someone would always wander over and ask if I was dealing.

I wasn't.

But I was broke. And to them I sounded it, so I took the hint. Gave them a hit.

Be open, be progressive, be happy for me, ya liberal cunts.

She retrieves two phones.

Two phones. Bop. Bop. My lifelines. It started with one personal and one business, but it blurred when I started getting busier. I started getting busier when I started getting better. Than you. I should probably get a third. But I like holding them at my hips like they're guns and I'm in a western. Pow-pow.

Okay.

She waits.

Okay.

And waits.

Okay.

And waits.

Okay.

And waits.

One rings.

About damn time. LET'S GO.

She picks up the phone.

Going nowhere. It's Mum. Un-ideal. Not a deal. Right let's get real.

The phone keeps ringing.

She'll just be asking questions about like, how I am and it's – boring. To lie to her.

She waits.

It rings out.

She was pissed about it at first. Which was disappointing because she was always like super feminist; single mum, only read me books by women and shit. A lot of Jacqueline Wilson. Me and her against the world against us. So, like I thought she'd have thought it was a bit bad ass. But she was all like… 'It's dangerous.' Why? What's dangerous about it? I'm not in like a gang thing. Not properly. It's just me and my gear and like… I approach it like a business. It is a fucking business. I run a good business and I don't need my mum to give me a tick in a box to succeed.

It'd be nice.

But I don't need it.

The other phone rings.

YES. FUCK YES.

You're about to see something special.

She clears her throat and picks up the phone.

The phones never stop. When she picks up one, the other rings.

Go for Lady Dealer –

See when it starts it's a domino run baby. Bustling energy flooding out my phone, into my body. Yeah sound. I feed on this shit. Like those little fish that nibble on your feet. Frantic frenzy but... natural. Nice. One second please. It is crack to me. I don't deal crack. I'm above that. Plus... you know. Bit vintage. All out, mate. I'm like the Oprah of drugs – you get some weed, and you get some weed, and you get some weed. Phone call after phone call, couriers dispatched, I should be on The fucking Apprentice. Yeah tomorrow's good.

It's non-stop and it's glorious.

If Clo knew what she'd walked out on she'd be furious.

This fire feels fucking excellent truth be told. Sure thing. Fuelling the population with what they need to get by. Why judge? I definitely do inhale. One does not have to set sail to their morals for this job, you just got to know how to navigate talking straight. Last one out the gate but first one over the finish line.

You alright?

It's honest.

You good?

It's relentlessly busy. This fizzy feeling in my balls, baby. It's like each time I answer a text or a call, I can see a wad of cash land on my lap. Screw Oprah man, I am the Santa Claus of dealing, fam. I'm healing the world one pill at a time. And what would you like for Christmas, little one? Some fucking ket? Absolutely.

It's an undeniable buzz straddling this horse. Hoping it takes me somewhere sunny with sand and a jug of sangria. Swimming in the sea of my legacy unfolding with every single ring of these two things. And –

The phones stop ringing.

And then sometimes there's a quiet half an hour. People in meetings or eating or whatever.

It's fine.

I just wait.

I'm fine.

I just wait.

Silence.

I think about calling Clo. Telling her she left her fairy lights, and the sight of them each morning is keeping me crippled in her pocket.

I don't.

I think about calling Mum and telling her I've not spoken to someone who isn't a client for six days.

I don't.

I just wait.

I'm fine.

I just wait.

Silence.

I scroll. Roll my thumb through images of women I can't breathe in enough to look like. Women at restaurants with lots of indoor plants. Women with kids, men with fish. Pretty Little Thing. Doomsday. Cults. Buzzfeed. Pinterest. Hotmail. Back to men with fish. TikTok. Consider learning one of them dances, decide I'm too old. Gmail. ASOS. Facebook. Got hooked when I was a kid, but now I literally just use it to judge all the people I went to school with. All got kids. Doomsday again. The *Guardian*. The *Daily Mail* gossip feed. Shame. Shame. Shame.

A knock at the door.

Ah, thank God.

Yeah, a couple of my regulars have my address. I'm not
nervous giving it out to be honest. I know too many people
who could kneecap any silly bugger. That's not necessarily
true. But instinctively, they think it is.

Good instincts. It's definitely a bit true.

Opening the door, I cannot contain my – disappointment. It's
Hugo.

I am a piranha for posh boys – they love me because they're
too fucking scared not to be on drugs, but they're also too
fucking scared to go to their local dealers, so... enter moi.
French again. Nailing it. Merci.

Bonjour, Hugo, come in, you slimy Tory twat.

Hugo wears deck shoes with no socks, and red chinos. That's
literally all you need to know about Hugo. I don't think he
has a last name. Hugo. He's like Cher but for Eton.

Yes. Sometimes visitations such as this give me the heebie-
jeebies. It is not lost on me that I am a woman alone with
a man that I don't know proper. But looking at Hugo – no
part of me is threatened. Feminist big balls lady dealer. It's
oddly nice, noticing the dynamic shift when he crosses from
outside to in. Out there he runs things. In here... it's mine.

Fuck refined. The world is mine. This world is mine.

<u>Here for the usual. The usge. Lil bit of the C word. The C
bomb. Nose candy and Mandy diet.</u>

He's off to take coke at the Jazz Café for a gig in the evening
and will inevitably slip his wedding ring off his finger and
into his pocket on the Northern line between Bank and
Camden.

Christ alive he's a pretentious twat. Twittering on about his
life like I asked about it. Like anybody has ever cared about
it. But suddenly he's handing me the cash and is making
his way back to my front door and I panic because it's all
happened far too fast for my liking and blurt out –

'Do you fancy a smoke?'

I don't know why I ask that, he's the last person I would want to smoke with and now he definitely thinks that I want to sleep with him despite the fact I am a fully fledged, card-carrying lesbian. And also if I wasn't, if Hugo approached me in a club, inevitably in a shit club, inevitably in a shit club in Clapham, I would deck him in the face.

I've got to get back to work.

Of course. Of course he does. Someone needs be stealing our money – she says without irony.

Right. Well. Have a good one.

I don't say it back. My only win. Which is kind of pathetic. But I'm fine, he's gone, and I'm fine.

My relief and embarrassment tangle up with each other in my stomach and as I close the door on him, I dart dramatically to the toilet to shit it out.

She sits on the toilet.

Excuse you mate. This is private.

Silence.

God you really deep your life when you're having a shit. Isaac Newton and the apple feels like a blatant lie – I bet the guy sat on the can, heard and splash and bang. Gravity.

Once, when I was a babe. Like sixteen. Back when stuff was vibrant sober, there was this girl that I went to school with called Tegan. Tegan was a tosser, but Tegan also had the richest parents – like the kind of rich that they're offering you pills and powder aged sixteen because they don't understand the passage of time – and they had this outhouse. The audacity – they called it a shed man, but it was the size of my whole fucking home. Bigger. And Tegan's parents would let her host these parties out there. Anyways, all that's mildly irrelevant. It is, to say, at one of these parties Tegan and two other brunettes I totally forget the names of,

convinced sixteen-year-old me that as a fellow female,
I HAD to accompany them to the bathroom. It's something
I just HAD to do. To gossip. To piss. To exist. So, I did what
I was told and sat in silence whilst they talked about boys
and took turns crying. THEN. One of the brunettes, clearly
done with her wee, the stream stops, and we just hear… plop.
We all try and act like it didn't happen but then… fart and a
bigger plop.

I threw up on the bath mat.

They all yelled at me. Like I'd done something wrong? Or
unexpected… or…

I didn't really understand that. I still don't. I don't think I
was supposed to throw up. But to be fair I don't think you're
meant to take a shit in front of people.

I dunno.

I mean, I do, I do know. I know that three other girls in that
bathroom did not throw up, and they all left friends. But it's
confusing because I really don't think I reacted abnormally.
Absolutely would've cleaned up the mess if they'd have
given me a chance to but what can you do when there's three
blonde girls yelling at you – it's one of their houses – and
the bath mat you've thrown up on is worth more than your
feelings. Who's healing that?

Was sort of the first inkling that I wasn't built for it… none
of it came easy with these people around me like… like
everyone learnt the rules on a day I bunked.

Why hasn't my phone rung?

She flushes.

She checks one phone.

Fuck.

She checks the other phone.

FUCK.

No, no, no, no, no. No, no, no, no, no. No, no, no, no, no.

She runs about manically for a charger.

NO.

She finds one, plugs it in, and pops it in her phone.

She waits.

Oooh tense.

Nothing.

Fuck.

She tries the other one.

Fuck! They weren't... they were on like forty. Fuck. Fuck.
No, no, no, no, no. No, no, no, no, no. No, no, no, no, no. No,
no, no, no, no.

She thinks.

*She heads back over to the PA system from earlier and tries
it again.*

Nothing.

Interesting. It's coz it's daylight. Why would you notice a
power cut in daylight?

Back to...

Today is going to be the same.

Today is going to be the same.

Today is going to be the same because I am fine.

I am fine?

I am. I am. I am. I'm fine.

The sun's been creeping at my ankles for a few hours now
but with the realisation that it could be my only form of light
today, it feels sneakier. It feels more... looming. Luminous
painting the white walls yellow.

We had to do that book at uni. With the crazy bitch on all-fours and yellow walls. That is not happening to me. Not today. Today is going to be the same. It has to be. Else a girl might shit on a toilet in front of me and I might throw up and it might ruin my entire life. It might not though. It might not.

It dawns on me pretty quickly that even if I didn't have a power cut... even if I slipped and broke something... even if I cared... and my phones were charged; people call me, I don't call people.

The thought feels like a tumour and I make an executive decision to fuck it.

I want hash browns; I want them now – in and around my mouth. So a pilgrimage to Maccy D's seems both wise and necessary. I know the clothes I'm currently wearing scream unshowered, but I also know that at this moment in time, if I walk back into MY bedroom and see HER fairy lights, I will have an all-consuming breakdown. So I head out as I am... messy. Raw. Mine. Fine.

I live on a council estate in Camberwell. Well, I say Camberwell to the Hugos of the world, it's definitely Peckham. Now something people don't tend to understand about council estates is they are at once both so sparkling with life, and utterly fucking suffocating. But I like it. You know, in the quiet I can hear murmurs of conversations from the missionaries next door, or the little lad beneath me that thinks he's the next DJ Khaled. And at night the sirens whir loud just reminding you that the city's still there. The apocalypse hasn't happened. It's all still ticking over. Like that's comforting.

But as I descend through the epicentre of life that is a block of flats the fragments of company dissipate. I'm on the street on the way to food and there's none of that. It's just... dead air. It's not fair that the world can't care that I'm out on this pavement. Can't make something spectacular just happen to distract me from the fact that I'm out on this pavement.

My ribs are concaving, they're going to puncture something important. The notion should scare me, but without the world caring about me, it sounds kind of nice. Like letting a balloon go.

So.

I think of that as I walk to big yellow M. A withering helium balloon just getting closer and closer to the ground. Soft landing. Outstanding. Understanding. It sustains me, and here we are.

'Two hash browns please.'

My voice cracks. I haven't used it in a while.

It's afternoon?

To her, that is an adequate response. To me she's put two words together, neither of which have anything to do with hash browns, and thus – FUCKING THUS – I am deeply uninterested in trying to decipher them.

We're not serving the breakfast menu any more.

At least that's clearer.

Imagination burned by burn holes, I order a Big Mac. Because why try and be different. Why try. Why try and be. Why try. Why.

I sit down next to this child and his glee. I can see the Happy Meal's been discarded in favour of the little toy. Little boy can't be more than ten. Trying desperately to be eleven, or even ten and half but he is ten. Twat doesn't appreciate ten. If I could be that age again, I'd take note. I'd bank shit in my brain, knowing that one day all the days would be same. I think when I was ten, I asked questions. My response to everything 'Why?'

Eat your dinner. Why?

Say thank you. Why?

Make friends.

I'm good. I'm fine.

My Big Mac is gone. I don't remember eating it, but I definitely did because I feel ashamed of myself.

It's time to go. I know. I know that. That it's time. Got to get back to the grind, and the grinder, the space that is mine, but I find it hard to leave here. There are so many voices talking over one another with their mouths and hearts mega full. Fully immersed in being beings. I like that I can't pick a conversation out. They're just happening around me like a hug, and if I'm a mug for enjoying that so be it. It's shit not participating in the party, but at least I've showed up, you know? I showed up. Don't I get something for that?

No.

Time to go.

Back into the dead air and the beggars and the preachers and the noise that's just not nice.

I don't think I ever looked at this city like you're supposed to look at it; like it's a challenge. Like it's something to conquer. I don't leave SE15. You know what I mean? You go out of what you know, where's the boundaries, how far do you go. Romeo and Juliet that shit. Where does it stop? Tried it. Me, SE15, Clo, TW9. Like I needed a sign anyways, but –

It cuts you. When someone you love – like – wants you as you are because the thing you are is exactly what they shouldn't want. In fonts she's Helvetica and I'm Comic Sans. She's raging parties and I'm weeknight plans.

She's – she's a trust-fund darling and I'm a female drug dealer.

Hashtag girl boss … but you know – less shit. Or not. I get confused on which generation I am – I think millennials love it and Gen X think it's naff… I'm indifferent what does that make me? Sagittarius? I'll tell you what that makes me, a hashtag girl boss. Heads-up this ramble is all totally meaningless by the way, but I'm walking home, and if I stop for a moment, I'll have a panic attack, so we just got to get through this together, pals – Daniel Bedingfield style – and discuss the mundanities of social-media feminism, which isn't real feminism by the way, it's performative; but of course you do have to perform your feminism else it's just an idea and feminism isn't an idea it's an urgent necessity and OH THANK GOD FRONT DOOR.

I spaced out. No idea what I just said and probably don't stand by any of it. So yeah.

Keys in the front door. In my core I know inside doesn't make me happier, I know there's no more people inside than outside but at least inside... it's mine. My bedroom is mine. And I am fine.

I am fucking fine.

I am fine. I am fine. I am fine. Fuck. I am though? I am fine.

Ezra Collective's 'You Can't Steal My Joy' begins playing very quietly, like it's far away.

A teeny trickle of music slithers under the door of another world and out into mine. I don't recognise it but I know it. In my soul. Something stirs that hasn't circled my system for a while. Curiosity feels too simple for this sensation but maybe that's just because it's new again. Against my better judgement I lean into listening. It's speaking to me as if it knows who I am. Like it's trying to tell me who I am.

Who am I without my coffee?

Fool. Getting distracted. MUSIC IS POWER.

She charges into her flat and plugs in her phone to the charger.

Come on...

She waits.

No.

She tries the other one.

FUCK.

She lies on the floor exasperated. So angered she's close to tears.

I could've taken my charger to McDonald's, couldn't I?

She almost cries.

She stops.

Ezra Collective's 'You Can't Steal My Joy' begins again.

How is there music then? How is there –

You think what you think of me at this point. Perhaps you're partly impressed by my business prowess, and the pride I have in that makes me a tiger. Not some silly bitch who cries on the floor. My productivity will cause Clo's eventual anonymity, she will live in shame that she left me. ME. A tiger. A tightly wound, totally fuckable tiger.

A tiger on the hunt.

My sniffer nose knows where the music's coming from. I hate the word rough. I hate it. Because growing up we were rough. We were the house that kept the England flag up when the football tournament was over, and we were the house where the dogs lived outside. It's a disgusting word made for the elite to feel sexy and for the less-thans to feel... to feel. I hate it. But the music's coming from the rough flat below. Alright? I know this estate like a friend, but that does not make us friendly. There are rules on an estate, mainly don't call the cops under any circumstances, and don't talk to each other. A mother and her brother had the flat two down from me. Bred dogs. Someone called the pigs. They were gone in two weeks.

Tread carefully, Charly.

Who the fuck are you without your coffee?

Knock knock, who the fuck are you without your coffee.

'CAN YOU TURN IT DOWN? I SAID WHO THE FUCK
ARE YOU MAN CAN YOU TURN IT DOWN.'

Ezra Collective stops playing.

I am not greeted by a less-than. I stand here as a have-not and
am greeted with a have.

Why?

Hi.

I'm Charly, I live above ya.

They know. He says.

We know.

The silence that lingers after that suggests they don't like me.
I feel my spine lengthening into my brain and I don't know
how to stop it coming out my skull. So I try and think of a
word, any word, that I can say out loud and not sound insane.

Electric.

Understandably – bless – he asks 'What?'

Have you got electricity? Mine's gone and my phones are
dead.

He takes a beat to register 'are'. Yes, plural. Plonker. I take
a beat to register him, he's… big. Bursting out of his clothes
in a very pleasant way. A belly that says, 'I care about joy
more than anything.' His linen is swinging at the holes to
create this shape of a man that I could love if I did. Me and
him, off-grid in a platonic campervan and… what a man. He
totally hates me.

Can I come in? No. Oh. He says that a bit quick for my
liking. He's breaking my broken heart. Hard to admit a
stranger can do that but –

No electric.

Oh. Right. Okay. Yeah. Yeah.

The relief that floods through me unnerves me a little; how much power did I just give his acceptance of me, if I'm feeling this at the antithesis of that. That's not good. I could. I could stand and tell him every single thing there is to know about me. I want to be really brutally honest with him about so much mess.

I want to be as honest as I can.

I want to tell him when I was younger, I used to love sitting in the bathtub until the water drained out. Because at the beginning of things you're sat in a bubble bath. And at the end of things you're naked in damp bowl. That's it.

No metaphors, no usurping the original idea. That's it.

Tell him that sometimes I think as dealers, or men, or people, or aches, we do life a disservice by only seeking beauty in the most complicated of ways. It must be found in a metaphor or a simile; assonance or alliteration; it must be unexpected. The beauty is a punchline. But sitting naked and damp in an empty bath may have been the only time I was properly at ease.

Honestly?

I want to tell him that I endlessly scroll through Pinterest looking for the quote that will save my soul. Maybe if I read enough Rupi Kaur I'll learn to like my thighs. Some cursive over millennial pink could teach me how to accept my fingernails without a base coat, pastel colour, topcoat and cuticle cream. Maybe. Maybe the more I hear the word Hygge the less panic attacks I'll have. Perhaps if I chant 'throw kindness around like confetti,' men will look me in the eye instead of my breasts, and despite being genuinely repulsed by them, maybe I'll stop basing my value on that. Maybe *Catcher in the Rye* is the answer. Maybe. Tumblr tells me – against a floral background – to ask myself, 'If what you're doing today is getting you closer to where you want to be tomorrow?' But what if I can't get out of bed today. What if today the world's screaming only seems to be reverberating around my ears.

I want to tell him pure cold hard facts. Tell him I am a size eight all over; top, bottom and feet.

Tell him I am five foot four. Tell him I've never dyed my hair and I have five tattoos; one on my wrist, one on my ankle, one on my stomach and two on my vagina. I have a scar on my left knee from falling off a bike when I was eight, and two scars on my back from climbing trees. Tell him I was smiling when I got them. Tell him I have been in my body for twenty-eight years and tell him I have hated it for twenty-five.

Tell him people will call you rude when you call a spade a spade.

People will call you a bitch for rolling your eyes when you're supposed to smile.

People will call you a rude bitch for throwing up on a bath mat at a posh person's party.

People have called me a rude bitch.

People call me a rude bitch.

Tell him I am a rude bitch.

Tell him I am a tiger.

Tell him I've not taken a bath in a long while because who do I have to impress? Ask him who cares if I'm happy? Tell him I'm not happy.

Tell him I'm fine.

Tell him I'm totally fine.

Instead, I ask him how he's playing music with no electricity.

It's good right?

Unexpected. I hadn't thought about liking something in quite a while. Not my style. Attachment. Letting someone settle in my hatch? Hutch? Clutching onto the things you've pretended you have in common just to have someone consistency in your life. Yuck. Like how can that not suck but this music…

It's swirling. Creating a whirlpool where there's usually a clenched fist.

Yeah. It's nice. How're you playing it?

He invites me in. Inside this grin stretches across my organs, tickling underneath my skin. It feels like yellow. Thank God he's turned around else I'd look mental just stood smiling at him. I'd swim, as a kid, it feels like that. Forcing your limbs to save your life passively. Being invited in feels like that. Invited in.

The air in his home smells a bit like dick. Usually that'd induce this sicky feeling but I'm still reeling from the invitation of the century so, I'm good. Yeah. No, I'm good. History will not repeat itself. My Big Mac will not repeat itself.

I'm good.

I find myself stood in a room of men. Boys. All dressed like pound shop Morrisseys, and crowded around what I sincerely think is a wind-up boom box. One of them clocks me and simply states <u>Dealer</u>. I feel an urge to clarify Lady Dealer but I have manners. So, I just nod. Then he nods. We're both nodding. Noticing that once that stops, there's no conversation left. A theft of happiness has happened in this room, and by process of elimination, I am the culprit. Guilt in my fingertips, and shame in thumbprint.

Who is this?

<u>Ezra Collective</u>

I don't know them.

<u>No. You just play loud noise.</u>

These boys weren't raised right but I'm not after a fight so I bite my tongue. I could tell them if it weren't for Beastie Boys hybrid culture in music might not exist. Both. But I don't. I could tell them I play it loud so I can't hear the empty echoes of my home. But I don't. I could tell them that I need them. But I don't. I don't need anyone.

What kind of music is it?

Jazz.

Jazz feels like a peculiar party choice?

Jazz is a bunch of strangers creating something entirely new together, specifically for each other. And what is a party if not a collaboration?

Well shit.

These profound prats purposely pick the words that prickle against me like squeezing a hedgehog. There's no point trying to articulate why that's made me... feel. Things. Intentional or not, they've brought me to the brink of tears, and I fear they're lovely but not emotionally equipped to deal with a female drug dealer crying in their doorway. Who is? Who are you without your coffee?

Will you let me know? If your electric comes back?

Sure. You can stay.

Oh God.

Are you okay?

Oh God.

Yeah I am. I am fine.

Quick math. Four lads, an invite to stay and a Lady Dealer with nothing to say. So. Assess. Reassess. Reality check. They didn't even ask my name.

How much you after?

What?

I'm speaking in grams but they're hearing tongues. Too tired for them to pretend they're not looking for a jazz-based discount, so I discuss an intro offer. Talking with the flow I know I feel my height grow, the mastery I show. This is what I know. This is what I know. This is what I know. This is what I know.

So. Five?

Their eyes are getting narrower. Why are their eyes getting narrower? Can they not see me. I'm Charly. Heaven sent candy man fam. Why are their eyes the size of my self-esteem? What are they looking for? I'm offering the world at a heavily reduced price. I'm being nice.

<u>Mate, we're just asking you to hang?</u>

Oh. No. I can't. What if one of them needs to poo. What if a client needs you. I can't.

I'm fine. I just got it wrong. But that's fine.

I am fine. I am – I'm. Fuck.

I scramble out of that house and back into the bedroom that is mine. I'm fine?

She sees the fairy lights. She grabs them and wraps herself up in them frantically.

She works hard to steady her breath.

She breathes in for four. Holds it for four. Exhales for four.

You go somewhere when you breathe proper. Like your brain takes you to where you're meant to be. Like... floating. In an open sea; and not in a terrifying *Jaws* kind of way but just this expanse of peace. And look, I wish I was fucking fancy, but I'm not, I am queen of the Red Stripe... so when I breathe proper, like that, I just... I just see hash browns. I see myself eating hash browns and beans on a Sunday morning, with white toast, in the local greasy spoon, with a raging hangover... and... and...

She fiddles with the fairy lights.

Clo was rude in the way rich people are – charmingly. Chubby cheeks chose to champion me. Cheesy as that may be, she chose me. I'd only ever been picked by default before, so you can see why I'd fall hard into adoration.

It's never been effortless for me. To be. With people. In any capacity. The audacity to tell me that party is a collaboration like I'm not trying. All the time. Trying to stop myself

crying, drying my eyes to The Streets beats, telling myself
this girl-meets-city romcom will work out. It has to work
out. I have the dream, I have the dream on my shoulders.
Heavy. Being here. Having cash. I'd be lying if I said I didn't
like the cash. You'd be dying if I said I didn't like the cash.
I'm dying when I'm busy buying presents for people I don't
have. Frying another dinner for one. I'm trying. But as soon
as my day has begun, I know it will be the same.

Today should've been the same.

She made it different. Disrupted my 'the same' into her 'the
same' and I welcomed that so willingly. Wouldn't breathe
unless it felt like it was for her. Just hurling every inhale
and exhale towards her permission. A pointless endeavour
because you're only ever seeking your own but –

First time we fucked?

I was standing. Feet not quite shoulder width apart, still
a little narrower, making myself a little smaller, but I was
standing. My backbone long, maybe my neck is a little short.
But standing. Tentative under statue. Nervous fizz inside my
skeleton. And I just kept thinking –

Is she going to love me at the end of this? She doesn't have
to, I don't know the girl. There might be a thousand reasons
why we're standing opposite each other right now.

Is this a transaction or connection? Am I currency, and if so,
am I trading it or is she?

She doesn't have to love me at the end of this. She doesn't
have to love me at the end of this.

I think I know how I'm feeling and so I begin peeling my
T-shirt over my stomach.

A flicker.

She's spotted my tattoo. I think she likes it. This bodes well
as I have two on my vagina, and they've taken people by
surprise before. Slowly the fabric moves above my breasts.

Freeze.

I'm about to let this woman inside of me. And she doesn't have to love me at the end of this.

So long as I love me at the end of this.

She doesn't have to love me at the end of this, but she's got to love me during. Absolutely fine so long as she loves me during. I want her to make my spine bend into my heart. I don't need to come but it's nice to; I think just feeling okay is heavily underrated.

I want to feel like I'm dancing. Or feel like I do when I'm dancing. A rhythm flooding your consciousness until something's not quite the same any more. But that time has passed. That's what got us here in the first place.

My bra goes as I invite her to trace the edges of me. The insecurities and the strange hobbies that I hope she doesn't ask me about. The strange hobbies I hope she does ask about. The frayed hems of them bits of those parts of these feelings. I hadn't been paying much attention, but her trousers are off. So are mine. It happened without me looking. My life has a tendency to do that.

Naked, the weight of her and everything else is on top of me. She calls me beautiful and I'm not even sure I care if she means it because something inside turns warm as she says it. And we laugh as we pant and it is all sweat.

She doesn't have to love me at the end of this.

But I hope she does.

And I know how dangerous that is. So I would say it over and over again. I said it when we dated, I said it when we fucked, I said it between the lines of imaginary vows, I would've still been saying it when we were grey and old and holding hands in a home. She doesn't have to love me at the end of this. But fuck me imagine if she does.

I really wanted her to. I really, really wanted her to. I really, really wanted her.

I really –

I'm over her.

Today should've been the same.

Silence.

You learn to cope. You walk that tightrope for a while,
realising moping gets you nowhere. Moping tips the balance.
But bending your body to someone else, supposedly that's
what it's all about but…

And sometimes the thought occurs. There might be a day
where she doesn't even recall that I loved her once. And
that… So excuse me if I walk down memory lane hoping to
bump into her every once in a while but that's –

But I am fine.

But.

Silence.

WEED.

She exclaims this like it's the first thought she's ever had.

She rolls a joint.

People don't like to admit it but there's a consistency to
drugs. A dependable dependency. Depends how you look at
things, but it stings once you realise the high guys are the
sanest of the sane. And when you supply the high guys, then
you are sanity embodied. And would the embodiment of
sanity get down in the dumps? I think the fuck not.

Green gets a bad rep; envy, greed, Anne Boleyn's sleeves;
but my buds aren't bad at all. All the stories of bath-salt
loonies eating faces – Florida, always in Florida – I read
and I'm like, dude just have zoot. I mean also, you know,
get counselling and try to grow up more rich, but also… just
have a zoot. Zoom out. Way out. So far that you can't see
you. It's lovely. Like an empty tub.

A postcard arrives.

'Hey petal. Sun is shining here in Skegness. Come next time.
Mum x'

She lights up and smokes her joint.

See? So, she's just calling to talk about herself. Her holiday.
Her happiness. Her house sat empty like her daughter and
she sent a postcard. Can't care. Too tiring. The other fifty
per cent of me was gone before I could crawl. So when I
look up at my future I only get to see half of it. And it works
at Interflora and has a gaggle of younger friends who make
excuses for her drunken digressions because they get that she
inherited a shitstorm and she's trying. She's always trying too
hard. Why is she always trying too hard? Why am I –

My future told me firmly I'm wasting my degree. I'm not the
one holidaying in Skegness.

'Come next time. Mum x'

Be better next time, Mum. Be happier next time, Mum. Be
different next time, Mum. Try again in the next life, Mum.
You're all out of whack in this one, Mum. Be friendlier next
time, Mum. Be calmer next time, Mum. Be the daughter I
actually want next year, Mum. Come next time, because your
life is so God awful you clearly must want to escape it, Mum.
Change who you are next time, Mum.

I am fine.

I am fine as I am. I'm fine.

I am –

Silence.

I feel no shame about my job. I feel deep shame about my
life. My insides, the spiritual insides, they're crumbling all
the time. My soul is an eroding cliff, and my mind is the
house stood precariously on top of it. The view's stunning
but it comes with a price. Ready to topple. Willing it, even.
Because when you constantly feel like something's coming –
good or bad – you just want it to come. Get it done.

I am a breakdown waiting to happen. And that's somehow
worse than being broken.

I don't have friends.

I'm twenty-eight years old and I don't have a friend. I have an ex and a mum. How do you begin again if you've never begun?

And we live in this time of enlightened acceptance… With exceptions. You can be a gobby drug dealer and a working-class, socialist lesbian, but you can't be… this. This forest fire, this landfill, this… this.

Who the fuck are you without your coffee?

Who the fuck are you without your coffee?

Who the fuck am I without my coffee?

Who are you? I'm fine. Who are you? I'm fine. Who are you? I'm fine. I'M FINE. I'M FINE.

Knock knock.

I look at the clock. It clicks that clients might've been trying to call. Trying to care that I'm not there for them when they need me. I'm sorry. I'm so sorry. I'm so sorry, I'm so – then it dawns… they don't all know my address… the beginnings of stress as I descend the stairs to the door.

Don't be a serial killer, don't be a serial killer, don't be a serial killer.

Keith? I'm sorry, I don't know a Keith I think you have the wrong – Hugo sent you? Hugo's been – Hugo suggested me? Right.

The ache gets the better of me. I let him in.

The man looks like a bin, like a human trash can. I'm not trying to be rude, but, equally, he's not trying to look like a human being so – I'm not a douche about who I deal to. As long you pay, we're okay. But this guy has cornflakes in his beard, and I'm inclined to believe he didn't have them for breakfast, so what does that say? It says I'll keep my distance. His smell will be here long after he is: it not repugnant, but pleasant would be an undeserved compliment.

Neutral would be an undeserved compliment. The guy smells of fish.

So how'd you know Hugo?

<u>I'm his father.</u>

Oh. Now he smells like money that doesn't have to bathe to be impressive. Money that gets out of the tub immediately.

<u>He gave me your number. I tried calling but – so he gave me your address.</u>

Yes. My phones are dead.

Power cut.

Can't charge them.

<u>Right. Well, I'm sorry to just... appear.</u>

I'm not sorry he appeared. Taking me back to the same, like a beautiful but unfortunately-ponging knight in shining armour. A farmer? Potentially? They're all rich Tories. I bet he's got some stories. I'd kill for grandparents I could kneel at the feet of, and listen to them ramble about the history of a war they didn't fight in. Don't scare him away. Settle. Oh God, I'm still wrapped in fairy lights. He'll probably thinks I'm not alright, but he's made it better. Beautiful. Full. I try to casually shrug them off, but I'm learning pretty quickly there's no casual or subtle way to remove fairy lights from your body. They're a bit of a talking point.

<u>Why are you –</u>

Why are you. Why.

They're my ex's.

<u>Right.</u>

I threw a glass at her.

Silence.

You out tonight too? With Hugo?

What? No. No. I'm... I'm suffering a bit of writer's block.

Ah yeah, well, hash will sort that right out my man, my brain never stops. You are after – um – I've got a range of buds. What do you –

Poems. Occasional short fiction, but... poems.

I've never met a poet before. I don't think anyone has, it's not a real job. It's like saying you're a banjo teacher or a sommelier. We've heard of them, but you never meet one in real life. If someone introduced themselves to me with a firm handshake, and told me they were a banjo teacher, I'd run for the fucking hills. But here I am. And there's a poet in my living room.

And the poet's begun to cry. Soft. Not sobs, just tears tearing their way through his blinks. But they are there. You can't help but stare at a grown man crying. We're both dying inside because this is awkward, no matter how you look at it. And you do look at it. He's refusing to acknowledge it. He's just stopped breathing as these heavy beads of sorrow run down to his chin.

I'm ill-equipped.

Equally maybe I'm the best person in the world to be opposite him right now. Because I don't pity him. Clumsily communicating can't be the way forward, but... empathising? Criticising a poet for having emotions isn't a good look. Criticising a female drug dealer boss bitch isn't a good look.

He finally dabs the tops of his cheeks with the back of his hairy hand. I hunt for the only rope I know that can pull us out of this well.

She rolls a joint for him.

One pre-roll on the house.

The way he coughs and splutters like Seth Rogan actually makes me so happy. Happens to the best of us. Human. Almost.

So why poems?

He's struck. Stumped. Stupefied by my studying him. Pal, you can't tell people you're a poet and not expect follow-up questions. His face forms quizzically. And then he says:

Why drugs?

Cash.

Same.

We laugh at our lies. Surprised. Surprised that someone is asking why. That someone else wants to excavate exactness. Wants to seek articulation and nuance and wants to fucking know why. Why? Surprised civilised ceremonies of small talk are this... this.

Surprised that I do know the answer, but my throat is backed up. Blocked with the vomit of sixteen-year-old me locked in a toilet at a shit house party and three girls who never liked me, one of whom had just accidentally began a poo.

Why drugs?

Why drugs?

Because people need drugs. And thus, people need me. And I don't think I've ever been needed. Wanted. Won't wallow in that, but... do you know how exhausting it is to be pushing. Constantly. Pushing your words out. Pushing your eyes to the right focus. Pushing, pushing, pushing, probably particularly prevalent in people pandering to the notion of 'meant to'. I cannot fathom 'meant to'. I am meant to be having fun, my life is meant to have begun. But this isn't Disney. This is Camberwell. THIS IS PECKHAM AND MY LIFE ISN'T WHAT IT'S MEANT TO BE.

Nothing's good enough.

I'm not strong enough.

I am fine.

Why poems?

Silence.

And then –

<u>When I think of you I don't.</u>

<u>When I think of you, I think of a Turner painting. Chaos and calm bedfellows in the mind of a blind man.</u>

<u>When I think of you, I think of Hockney's splash. A perfect moment imperfectly captured forever.</u>

<u>When I think of you, I think of Van Gogh's sunflowers, vibrant in the moment but sad in the memory.</u>

<u>When I think of you, I think of the winding lines of age appearing around your eyes like Welsh valleys that better poets wrote better poetry about.</u>

<u>When I think of you, which I do oh so often, I don't.</u>

<u>When I think of you, I think of everything.</u>

<u>Because that is what you were.</u>

Silence.

<u>You?</u>

Silence.

If I collapse at mile twenty-three

Wait for me

I know you're not meant to say that

I know you're meant to say carry on without me

But don't do that.

I want to feel our bellies hitting that red ribbon in unison.

CHARLY *takes a big breath.*

Keith? I think I'm really fucking lonely.

Suddenly, with a heart-stopping jolt, Sabotage – Beastie Boys blasts out, picking up where it left off.

THE NOISE I HAVE BEEN CRAVING TO SAVE ME
NOW SEEMS… OVERWHELMING. TOO MUCH. MUCH
TO MY DISMAY I MAY, I MAY – FUCK – I MAY HAVE
GOTTEN MYSELF WRONG. HOW CAN I EXPECT
ANYTHING FROM ANYONE WHEN I CAN'T EVEN
DO ME RIGHT. THERE'S NO MANUAL ON HOW TO
MOVE THROUGH LIFE YOU'RE JUST EXPECTED TO
DO IT RIGHT THE FIRST TIME AND THAT SEEMS
LIKE A REALLY REALLY SHIT SYSTEM TO ME AND
TO KEITH TOO I ASSUME. I MEAN THE GUY NAMED
HIS CHILD HUGO SO HE KNOWS ABOUT MISTAKES.
I CAN'T. I CAN'T DO IT.

I AM FINE. I AM FEELING FINE. I AM FEELING. I
AM – I AM NOT GOING TO BE SAVED BY A MAN
WITH HAIR GROWING ALL THE WAY THROUGH
HIM. PROBABLY ALL KNOTTY AND MATTED ON HIS
CHEST. HIS CHEST WHERE HE ONCE WOULD'VE
LAIN HIS SON'S HEAD. HIS CHEST BUILT FOR REST
THAT I DO NOT NEED BECAUSE I AM FINE. WHY IS
HE LOOKING AT ME?

I AM FINE. I AM FINE. I AM? I AM F– WHAT? WHY? I
AM – WHY AM I FINE? I'M FINE. I AM FINE. I – I AM. I
AM – I – YOU DON'T – I AM FINE.

I know.

WHAT?

I KNOW.

THEY STAND IN THE NOISE.

She turns the music off by ripping the cord from the plug.

They stand in the silence.

Long, long silence.

Did I say the wrong thing?

You didn't say anything.

Well I –

You didn't say anything.

They stand in the silence.

Your son is my least favourite breed of man.

<u>Mine too. You're allowed to cry, you know?</u>

Yes, I do know I'm allowed to cry in my own home.

<u>Do you want to?</u>

No. Maybe. I don't know.

<u>You don't know?</u>

I can't.

<u>Why?</u>

You're not my – stop it.

I'm willing myself to, but the tears just aren't coming. I want to sob. I want my shoulders to heave and to taste my own snot, but it's not right. What I feel. It's not as explosive as that. It's just this continuously present hurt. Sometimes I think there's this feeling – this emotion – that only women feel and there's no word for it because men never named it… so we can't articulate it. We've never been able to articulate it and so at some point we convinced ourselves it just didn't even exist. But it does. It is there. It just sits in us. Like this thing that's so impossible to describe. No words are right; it's not quite sadness and it's not quite unfulfillment. And we have absolutely no idea if it's our fault or if it's the world's fault or if it's got any sort of cure. It's just a feeling that's not a feeling, that doesn't exist but is very there. A thread from cradle to grave of something that just hurts a tiny bit for absolutely no reason. All over. But… no it doesn't hurt, that's not right. This is what I mean I have no idea how it feels or what it's called… it's just – there. Every second of every day. Just. There.

I just feel sad all the time. Even when I'm nearly happy. Just. There.

There's no point in trying to articulate that to Keith. He'd try.
Nice guy. But. Of course. But. And he's not my dad.

You're not my dad.

<u>I know.</u>

Can you stop saying you know? I get it; you're smart, you're
old, you're rich, you know everything. Actually, yeah, you
could – could you – can you – I want you to leave.

<u>I've not paid.</u>

It's fine.

<u>You want me to leave without paying?</u>

Yes, you fucking parrot.

<u>Why?</u>

CHARLY *tries. She tries so, so hard.*

Because I threw up at Tegan's house party when I was
sixteen and I should've swallowed it.

There is a long pause.

<u>Ah. I understand entirely.</u>

Keith leaves.

Keith leaves with his buds. Keith buds with his leaves.
Leaving me lost in the –

CHARLY *stands so alone.*

Fuck it.

CHARLY *gives up on poetry.*

It is so quiet, it is its own noise.

She checks her phones.

Charging.

She stands in the silence.

Her phones begin to ring.

She can't pick it up. It rings out.

Today I have spoken to a poet, a fast-food employee, a posh prat and a bunch of boys, that I have never spoken to before, and I feel fucking knackered.

It is so overrated, talking to new people. It is so underrated being in silence with the person you love and feeling nothing drastic. Feeling nothing at all. Feeling numb. It is so underrated feeling numb.

Perhaps that's not love, but then the really underrated thing is being content. And perhaps that is.

What I'd give to be Tegan for a day. To be a girl that can host parties. A girl that can bring people to her. A girl that can do it… all. A girl with people that care about her. But I'm not.

I'm fucking not.

I'm nothing.

I'm Charly.

I'm a drug dealer.

My ex is called Clo. I'm fully aware she is not the love of my life, and yet think she might be what the whole thing revolves around.

All I have left of her love are some fairy lights I don't even like.

My mum is disappointed in the lack of me inside me.

I find navigating normal rooms totally impossible.

I am really good at my job.

I desperately want to take a bath and sit in it until all the water runs out.

The phone begins to ring again.

I thought today was going to be the same.

Then the other.

I really thought today was going to be the same.

She picks up the phone.

Go for Lady Dea–

Oh. Mum. Hi.

Yeah, sorry I'd just got up.

That's good.

Yeah I did, it literally just arrived.

Cool.

I'm glad.

Yeah?

Yeah.

Maybe. I don't know what I'm doing a year from now, you know? Maybe. It's –

Yeah.

Well that's good.

Was it?

Nice.

Oh just working. The usual. Just, me and the ol' usual. Very unexciting. How are you?

Nice.

A pause.

Me?

Yeah, I'm fine.

She plugs in the fairy lights and their light grows.

There is also a hum of weed.

I am fine. I am fine. I am fine. I am fine. I am fine. I am fine. I am fine. I am fine. I am fine. I am fine. I am fine. I am fine.

I am fine. I am fine. I am fine. I am fine. I am fine. I am fine.
I am fine. I am fine. I am fine. I am fine. I am fine. I am fine.
I am fine. I am fine. I am fine. I am fine. I am fine. I am fine.
I am fine. I am fine. I am fine. I am fine. I am fine. I am fine.

And keeps growing and glowing.

The other phone begins to ring.

*There is also a baby crying. There is also the bitter taste of
bile. There is also the stench of decade-old-vomit. There is
also the cackle of teenage laughter. There are also friends
that aren't friendly.*

I am fine. I am fine. I am fine. I am fine. I am fine. I am fine.
I am fine. I am fine. I am fine. I am fine. I am fine. I am fine.
I am fine. I am fine. I am fine. I am fine. I am fine. I am fine.
I am fine. I am fine. I am fine. I am fine. I am fine. I am fine.
I am fine. I am fine. I am fine. I am fine. I am fine. I am fine.
I am fine. I am fine. I am fine. I am fine. I am fine. I am fine.
I am fine. I am fine. I am fine. I am fine. I am fine. I am fine.
I am fine. I am fine. I am fine. I am fine. I am fine. I am fine.
I am fine. I am fine. I am fine. I am fine. I am fine. I am fine.

*Their light fills up the whole room to the point you are
blinded by it.*

Her other phone begins to ring.

*There is also the abyss of a lover. There is also the phrase
'class-traitor'. There is also a father who doesn't exist. There
is also a mother who exists a bit too much. There is also a
country that genuinely sucks balls. There is also the sound of
cash rubbing against cash. There are also unsayable words.
There is also the NHS.*

I am fine. I am fine. I am fine. I am fine. I am fine. I am fine.
I am fine. I am fine. I am fine. I am fine. I am fine. I am fine.
I am fine. I am fine. I am fine. I am fine. I am fine. I am fine.
I am fine. I am fine. I am fine. I am fine. I am fine. I am fine.
I am fine. I am fine. I am fine. I am fine. I am fine. I am fine.
I am fine. I am fine. I am fine. I am fine. I am fine. I am fine.
I am fine. I am fine. I am fine. I am fine. I am fine. I am fine.
I am fine. I am fine. I am fine. I am fine. I am fine. I am fine.

I am fine. I am fine. I am fine. I am fine. I am fine. I am fine.
I am fine. I am fine. I am fine. I am fine. I am fine. I am fine.
I am fine. I am fine. I am fine. I am fine. I am fine. I am fine.
I am fine. I am fine. I am fine. I am fine. I am fine. I am fine.
I am fine. I am fine. I am fine. I am fine. I am fine. I am fine.

She approaches the tower of clothes and yanks the pastel-yellow sweater from it.

The tower falls.

There is also climate change, income inequality and the fact that that singer cheated on that actor. There is also Ezra Collective. There is also an argument five doors down. There is also the noise of a fast-food chain that only exists in that fast food chain.

I am fine. I am fine. I am fine. I am fine. I am fine. I am fine.
I am fine. I am fine. I am fine. I am fine. I am fine. I am fine.
I am fine. I am fine. I am fine. I am fine. I am fine. I am fine.
I am fine. I am fine. I am fine. I am fine. I am fine. I am fine.
I am fine. I am fine. I am fine. I am fine. I am fine. I am fine.
I am fine. I am fine. I am fine. I am fine. I am fine. I am fine.
I am fine. I am fine. I am fine. I am fine. I am fine. I am fine.
I am fine. I am fine. I am fine. I am fine. I am fine. I am fine.
I am fine. I am fine. I am fine. I am fine. I am fine. I am fine.
I am fine. I am fine. I am fine. I am fine. I am fine. I am fine.
I am fine. I am fine. I am fine. I am fine. I am fine. I am fine.
I am fine. I am fine. I am fine. I am fine. I am fine. I am fine.
I am fine. I am fine. I am fine. I am fine. I am fine. I am fine.
I am fine. I am fine. I am fine. I am fine. I am fine. I am fine.
I am fine. I am fine. I am fine. I am fine. I am fine. I am fine.

The phone rings and rings and rings.

There are also too many people. There is also China's solution to that. There is also your phone. There is also the news. There is also fast fashion. There is also your bank.

I am fine. I am fine. I am fine. I am fine. I am fine. I am fine.
I am fine. I am fine. I am fine. I am fine. I am fine. I am fine.
I am fine. I am fine. I am fine. I am fine. I am fine. I am fine.

I am fine. I am fine. I am fine. I am fine. I am fine. I am fine.
I am fine. I am fine. I am fine. I am fine. I am fine. I am fine.
I am fine. I am fine. I am fine. I am fine. I am fine. I am fine.
I am fine. I am fine. I am fine. I am fine. I am fine. I am fine.
I am fine. I am fine. I am fine. I am fine. I am fine. I am fine.
I am fine. I am fine. I am fine. I am fine. I am fine. I am fine.
I am fine. I am fine. I am fine. I am fine. I am fine. I am fine.
I am fine. I am fine. I am fine. I am fine. I am fine. I am fine.
I am fine. I am fine. I am fine. I am fine. I am fine. I am fine.
I am fine. I am fine. I am fine. I am fine. I am fine. I am fine.
I am fine. I am fine. I am fine. I am fine. I am fine. I am fine.
I am fine. I am fine. I am fine. I am fine. I am fine. I am fine.
I am fine. I am fine. I am fine. I am fine. I am fine. I am fine.
I am fine. I am fine. I am fine. I am fine. I am fine. I am fine.
I am fine. I am fine. I am fine. I am fine. I am fine. I am fine.

There is also more.

I am fine. I am fine. I am fine. I am fine. I am fine. I am fine.
I am fine. I am fine. I am fine. I am fine. I am fine. I am fine.
I am fine. I am fine. I am fine. I am fine. I am fine. I am fine.
I am fine. I am fine. I am fine. I am fine. I am fine. I am fine.
I am fine. I am fine. I am fine. I am fine. I am fine. I am fine.
I am fine. I am fine. I am fine. I am fine. I am fine. I am fine.
I am fine. I am fine. I am fine. I am fine. I am fine. I am fine.
I am fine. I am fine. I am fine. I am fine. I am fine. I am fine.
I am fine. I am fine. I am fine. I am fine. I am fine. I am fine.
I am fine. I am fine. I am fine. I am fine. I am fine. I am fine.
I am fine. I am fine. I am fine. I am fine. I am fine. I am fine.
I am fine. I am fine. I am fine. I am fine. I am fine. I am fine.
I am fine. I am fine. I am fine. I am fine. I am fine. I am fine.
I am fine. I am fine. I am fine. I am fine. I am fine. I am fine.
I am fine. I am fine. I am fine. I am fine. I am fine. I am fine.
I am fine. I am fine. I am fine. I am fine. I am fine. I am fine.
I am fine. I am fine. I am fine. I am fine. I am fine. I am fine.
I am fine. I am fine. I am fine. I am fine. I am fine. I am fine.
I am fine. I am fine. I am fine. I am fine. I am fine. I am fine.
I am fine. I am fine. I am fine. I am fine. I am fine. I am fine.
I am fine. I am fine. I am fine. I am fine. I am fine. I am fine.

There is also more. There is also more. There is also more.
There is also more. There is also more. There is also more.
There is also more. There is also more. There is also more.
There is also more. There is also more. There is also more.
There is also more. There is also more. There is also more.
There is also more. There is also more. There is also more.

I am fine. I am fine. I am fine. I am fine. I am fine. I am fine.
I am fine. I am fine. I am fine. I am fine. I am fine. I am fine.
I am fine. I am fine. I am fine. I am fine. I am fine. I am fine.
I am fine. I am fine. I am fine. I am fine. I am fine. I am fine.
I am fine. I am fine. I am fine. I am fine. I am fine. I am fine.
I am fine. I am fine. I am fine. I am fine. I am fine. I am fine.
I am fine. I am fine. I am fine. I am fine. I am fine. I am fine.
I am fine. I am fine. I am fine. I am fine. I am fine. I am fine.
I am fine. I am fine. I am fine. I am fine. I am fine. I am fine.
I am fine. I am fine. I am fine. I am fine. I am fine. I am fine.
I am fine. I am fine. I am fine. I am fine. I am fine. I am fine.
I am fine. I am fine. I am fine. I am fine. I am fine. I am fine.
I am fine. I am fine. I am fine. I am fine. I am fine. I am fine.
I am fine. I am fine. I am fine. I am fine. I am fine. I am fine.
I am fine. I am fine. I am fine. I am fine. I am fine. I am fine.
I am fine. I am fine. I am fine. I am fine. I am fine. I am fine.
I am fine. I am fine. I am fine. I am fine. I am fine. I am fine.
I am fine. I am fine. I am fine. I am fine. I am fine. I am fine.
I am fine. I am fine. I am fine. I am fine. I am fine. I am fine.
I am fine. I am fine. I am fine. I am fine. I am fine. I am fine.
I am fine. I am fine. I am fine. I am fine. I am fine. I am fine.
I am fine. I am fine. I am fine. I am fine. I am fine. I am fine.
I am fine. I am fine. I am fine. I am fine. I am fine. I am fine.
I am fine. I am fine. I am fine. I am fine. I am fine. I am fine.
I am fine. I am fine. I am fine. I am fine. I am fine. I am fine.

There is also a mum who sends her postcards.

I am fine. I am fine. I am fine. I am fine. I am fine. I am fine.
I am fine. I am fine. I am fine. I am fine. I am fine. I am fine.
I am fine. I am fine. I am fine. I am fine. I am fine. I am fine.
I am fine. I am fine. I am fine. I am fine. I am fine. I am fine.
I am fine. I am fine. I am fine. I am fine. I am fine. I am fine.
I am fine. I am fine. I am fine. I am fine. I am fine. I am fine.

I am fine. I am fine. I am fine. I am fine. I am fine. I am fine.
I am fine. I am fine. I am fine. I am fine. I am fine. I am fine.
I am fine. I am fine. I am fine. I am fine. I am fine. I am fine.
I am fine. I am fine. I am fine. I am fine. I am fine. I am fine.
I am fine. I am fine. I am fine. I am fine. I am fine. I am fine.
I am fine. I am fine. I am fine. I am fine. I am fine. I am fine.
I am fine. I am fine. I am fine. I am fine. I am fine. I am fine.
I am fine. I am fine. I am fine. I am fine. I am fine. I am fine.
I am fine. I am fine. I am fine. I am fine. I am fine. I am fine.
I am fine. I am fine. I am fine. I am fine. I am fine. I am fine.
I am fine. I am fine. I am fine. I am fine. I am fine. I am fine.
I am fine. I am fine. I am fine. I am fine. I am fine. I am fine.
I am fine. I am fine. I am fine. I am fine. I am fine. I am fine.
I am fine. I am fine. I am fine. I am fine. I am fine. I am fine.
I am fine. I am fine. I am fine. I am fine. I am fine. I am fine.
I am fine. I am fine. I am fine. I am fine. I am fine. I am fine.
I am fine. I am fine. I am fine. I am fine. I am fine. I am fine.
I am fine. I am fine. I am fine. I am fine. I am fine. I am fine.
I am fine. I am fine. I am fine. I am fine. I am fine. I am fine.
I am fine. I am fine. I am fine. I am fine. I am fine. I am fine.
I am fine. I am fine. I am fine. I am fine. I am fine. I am fine.
I am fine. I am fine. I am fine. I am fine. I am fine. I am fine.

There is also a neighbour who invited her to stay.

I am fine. I am fine. I am fine. I am fine. I am fine. I am fine.
I am fine. I am fine. I am fine. I am fine. I am fine. I am fine.
I am fine. I am fine. I am fine. I am fine. I am fine. I am fine.
I am fine. I am fine. I am fine. I am fine. I am fine. I am fine.
I am fine. I am fine. I am fine. I am fine. I am fine. I am fine.
I am fine. I am fine. I am fine. I am fine. I am fine. I am fine.
I am fine. I am fine. I am fine. I am fine. I am fine. I am fine.
I am fine. I am fine. I am fine. I am fine. I am fine. I am fine.
I am fine. I am fine. I am fine. I am fine. I am fine. I am fine.
I am fine. I am fine. I am fine. I am fine. I am fine. I am fine.
I am fine. I am fine. I am fine. I am fine. I am fine. I am fine.
I am fine. I am fine. I am fine. I am fine. I am fine. I am fine.
I am fine. I am fine. I am fine. I am fine. I am fine. I am fine.
I am fine. I am fine. I am fine. I am fine. I am fine. I am fine.
I am fine. I am fine. I am fine. I am fine. I am fine. I am fine.
I am fine. I am fine. I am fine. I am fine. I am fine. I am fine.
I am fine. I am fine. I am fine. I am fine. I am fine. I am fine.

I am fine. I am fine. I am fine. I am fine. I am fine. I am fine.
I am fine. I am fine. I am fine. I am fine. I am fine. I am fine.
I am fine. I am fine. I am fine. I am fine. I am fine. I am fine.
I am fine. I am fine. I am fine. I am fine. I am fine. I am fine.
I am fine. I am fine. I am fine. I am fine. I am fine. I am fine.
I am fine. I am fine. I am fine. I am fine. I am fine. I am fine.
I am fine. I am fine. I am fine. I am fine. I am fine. I am fine.
I am fine. I am fine. I am fine. I am fine. I am fine. I am fine.
I am fine. I am fine. I am fine. I am fine. I am fine. I am fine.
I am fine. I am fine. I am fine. I am fine. I am fine. I am fine.
I am fine. I am fine. I am fine. I am fine. I am fine. I am fine.
I am fine. I am fine. I am fine. I am fine. I am fine. I am fine.
I am fine. I am fine. I am fine. I am fine. I am fine. I am fine.
I am fine. I am fine. I am fine. I am fine. I am fine. I am fine.

There is also a man called Keith who asked her why.

I am fine. I am fine. I am fine. I am fine. I am fine. I am fine.
I am fine. I am fine. I am fine. I am fine. I am fine. I am fine.
I am fine. I am fine. I am fine. I am fine. I am fine. I am fine.
I am fine. I am fine. I am fine. I am fine. I am fine. I am fine.
I am fine. I am fine. I am fine. I am fine. I am fine. I am fine.
I am fine. I am fine. I am fine. I am fine. I am fine. I am fine.
I am fine. I am fine. I am fine. I am fine. I am fine. I am fine.
I am fine. I am fine. I am fine. I am fine. I am fine. I am fine.
I am fine. I am fine. I am fine. I am fine. I am fine. I am fine.
I am fine. I am fine. I am fine. I am fine. I am fine. I am fine.
I am fine. I am fine. I am fine. I am fine. I am fine. I am fine.
I am fine. I am fine. I am fine. I am fine. I am fine. I am fine.
I am fine. I am fine. I am fine. I am fine. I am fine. I am fine.
I am fine. I am fine. I am fine. I am fine. I am fine. I am fine.
I am fine. I am fine. I am fine. I am fine. I am fine. I am fine.
I am fine. I am fine. I am fine. I am fine. I am fine. I am fine.
I am fine. I am fine. I am fine. I am fine. I am fine. I am fine.
I am fine. I am fine. I am fine. I am fine. I am fine. I am fine.
I am fine. I am fine. I am fine. I am fine. I am fine. I am fine.
I am fine. I am fine. I am fine. I am fine. I am fine. I am fine.
I am fine. I am fine. I am fine. I am fine. I am fine. I am fine.
I am fine. I am fine. I am fine. I am fine. I am fine. I am fine.
I am fine. I am fine. I am fine. I am fine. I am fine. I am fine.

I am fine. I am fine. I am fine. I am fine. I am fine. I am fine.
I am fine. I am fine. I am fine. I am fine. I am fine. I am fine.
I am fine. I am fine. I am fine. I am fine. I am fine. I am fine.
I am fine. I am fine. I am fine. I am fine. I am fine. I am fine.
I am fine. I am fine. I am fine. I am fine. I am fine. I am fine.
I am fine. I am fine. I am fine. I am fine. I am fine. I am fine.
I am fine. I am fine. I am fine. I am fine. I am fine. I am fine.

There is also hope. Maybe.

I am fine. I am fine. I am fine. I am fine. I am fine. I am fine.
I am fine. I am fine. I am fine. I am fine. I am fine. I am fine.
I am fine. I am fine. I am fine. I am fine. I am fine. I am fine.
I am fine. I am fine. I am fine. I am fine. I am fine. I am fine.
I am fine. I am fine. I am fine. I am fine. I am fine. I am fine.
I am fine. I am fine. I am fine. I am fine. I am fine. I am fine.
I am fine. I am fine. I am fine. I am fine. I am fine. I am fine.
I am fine. I am fine. I am fine. I am fine. I am fine. I am fine.
I am fine. I am fine. I am fine. I am fine. I am fine. I am fine.
I am fine. I am fine. I am fine. I am fine. I am fine. I am fine.
I am fine. I am fine. I am fine. I am fine. I am fine. I am fine.
I am fine. I am fine. I am fine. I am fine. I am fine. I am fine.
I am fine. I am fine. I am fine. I am fine. I am fine. I am fine.
I am fine. I am fine. I am fine. I am fine. I am fine. I am fine.
I am fine. I am fine. I am fine. I am fine. I am fine. I am fine.
I am fine. I am fine. I am fine. I am fine. I am fine. I am fine.
I am fine. I am fine. I am fine. I am fine. I am fine. I am fine.
I am fine. I am fine. I am fine. I am fine. I am fine. I am fine.
I am fine. I am fine. I am fine. I am fine. I am fine. I am fine.
I am fine. I am fine. I am fine. I am fine. I am fine. I am fine.
I am fine. I am fine. I am fine. I am fine. I am fine. I am fine.
I am fine. I am fine. I am fine. I am fine. I am fine. I am fine.
I am fine. I am fine. I am fine. I am fine. I am fine. I am fine.
I am fine. I am fine. I am fine. I am fine. I am fine. I am fine.
I am fine. I am fine. I am fine. I am fine. I am fine. I am fine.
I am fine. I am fine. I am fine. I am fine. I am fine. I am fine.
I am fine. I am fine. I am fine. I am fine. I am fine. I am fine.
I am fine. I am fine. I am fine. I am fine. I am fine. I am fine.

I am fine. I am fine. I am fine. I am fine. I am fine. I am fine.
I am fine. I am fine. I am fine. I am fine. I am fine. I am fine.
I am fine. I am fine. I am fine. I am fine. I am fine. I am fine.

JUST KEEP FUCKING GOING, CHARLY, JUST KEEP
FUCKING GOING UNTIL IT IS TRUE.

I am fine. I am fine. I am fine. I am fine. I am fine. I am fine.
I am fine. I am fine. I am fine. I am fine. I am fine. I am fine.
I am fine. I am fine. I am fine. I am fine. I am fine. I am fine.
I am fine. I am fine. I am fine. I am fine. I am fine. I am fine.
I am fine. I am fine. I am fine. I am fine. I am fine. I am fine.
I am fine. I am fine. I am fine. I am fine. I am fine. I am fine.
I am fine. I am fine. I am fine. I am fine. I am fine. I am fine.
I am fine. I am fine. I am fine. I am fine. I am fine. I am fine.
I am fine. I am fine. I am fine. I am fine. I am fine. I am fine.
I am fine. I am fine. I am fine. I am fine. I am fine. I am fine.
I am fine. I am fine. I am fine. I am fine. I am fine. I am fine.
I am fine. I am fine. I am fine. I am fine. I am fine. I am fine.
I am fine. I am fine. I am fine. I am fine. I am fine. I am fine.
I am fine. I am fine. I am fine. I am fine. I am fine. I am fine.
I am fine. I am fine. I am fine. I am fine. I am fine. I am fine.
I am fine. I am fine. I am fine. I am fine. I am fine. I am fine.
I am fine. I am fine. I am fine. I am fine. I am fine. I am fine.
I am fine. I am fine. I am fine. I am fine. I am fine. I am fine.
I am fine. I am fine. I am fine. I am fine. I am fine. I am fine.
I am fine. I am fine. I am fine. I am fine. I am fine. I am fine.
I am fine. I am fine. I am fine. I am fine. I am fine. I am fine.
I am fine. I am fine. I am fine. I am fine. I am fine. I am fine.
I am fine. I am fine. I am fine. I am fine. I am fine. I am fine.
I am fine. I am fine. I am fine. I am fine. I am fine. I am fine.
I am fine. I am fine. I am fine. I am fine. I am fine. I am fine.
I am fine. I am fine. I am fine. I am fine. I am fine. I am fine.
I am fine. I am fine. I am fine. I am fine. I am fine. I am fine.
I am fine. I am fine. I am fine. I am fine. I am fine. I am fine.
I am fine. I am fine. I am fine. I am fine. I am fine. I am fine.
I am fine. I am fine. I am fine. I am fine. I am fine. I am fine.
I am fine. I am fine. I am fine. I am fine. I am fine. I am fine.
I am fine. I am fine. I am fine. I am fine. I am fine. I am fine.
I am fine. I am fine. I am fine. I am fine. I am fine. I am fine.
I am fine. I am fine. I am fine. I am fine. I am fine. I am fine.

I am fine. I am fine.

You can barely make out CHARLY, *as she stares into the sun.*

I am fine.

Blackout.

The End.

A Nick Hern Book

Lady Dealer first published in Great Britain as a paperback original in 2023 by Nick Hern Books Limited, The Glasshouse, 49a Goldhawk Road, London W12 8QP, in association with Grace Dickson Productions

Lady Dealer copyright © 2023 Martha Watson Allpress

Martha Watson Allpress has asserted her right to be identified as the author of this work

Cover photography by Harry Elletson

Designed and typeset by Nick Hern Books, London
Printed in Great Britain by Mimeo Ltd, Huntingdon, Cambridgeshire PE29 6XX

A CIP catalogue record for this book is available from the British Library

ISBN 978 1 83904 264 5

www.nickhernbooks.co.uk/environmental-policy

www.nickhernbooks.co.uk

facebook.com/nickhernbooks

twitter.com/nickhernbooks